# EURO
## HISTORY & DEVELOPMENT

## Ian Moncrief-Scott

Information Management Solutions Limited

ISLE OF MAN

The author Ian Moncrief-Scott has asserted his right under the Copyright, Designs and Patents Act 1988 to be identified as the author of this work.

Copyright. © I. Moncrief-Scott 2021

All rights reserved. No part of this publication may be produced in any form or by any means - graphic, electronic, or mechanical, including photocopying, recording, taping, or information storage and retrieval systems - without the prior permission in writing of the publishers.

The publishers make no representation, express or implied, regarding the accuracy of the information contained in this book and cannot accept any legal responsibility for any errors or omissions that may take place.

A CIP catalogue record for this book is available from the British Library.

Published by Information Management Solutions Limited, 17 Howe Road, Onchan, Isle of Man, IM3 2BB.

Printed, bound and distributed by IngramSpark.

Book Layout © 2017 BookDesignTemplates.com

Superhero Peg Image: Besjunior/Shutterstock.com

Cover Source by Tanja Prokop of BookDesignTemplates.com

**EURO: HISTORY & DEVELOPMENT – 2nd ed.**
ISBN 9781903467053

The Publishers have been requested by the author to acknowledge the direct and indirect contributions to this book by:

The Bank of England
The Bank of England Museum
European Monetary Institute
European Central Bank

This book is dedicated to
start-up entrepreneurs.


The front cover depicts
ordinary wooden clothes pegs dressed as
Super Heroes.


**All start-up entrepreneurs are
ordinary people
turning into Super Heroes!**

# CONTENTS

EURO .................................................................................. 1
OTHER BOOKS BY THE AUTHOR ................................. 9
FORTHCOMING BOOKS BY THE AUTHOR ................ 11

# EURO

Arguably, the most significant change to the world's money markets took place on 1 January 1999. Eleven nations of Europe replaced their currency with the new Euro. The move spelled the end of the Franc and the Mark.

Great Britain, though not joining initially, had not ruled out membership should suitable economic conditions prevail. Ultimately, the step could signal the end of dozens of independent countries and signify the United States of Europe.

Article 105a (1) of the Treaty on European Union, popularly known as the Maastricht Treaty, gave the European Central Bank exclusive right to authorise the issue of banknotes and coin within the participating Member States.

Also established by the Treaty, the European Monetary Institute Council (EMI), formed by the National Central Banks, has two main tasks. Contribute to reaching Stage III of Economic and Monetary Union (EMU), and prepare the European System of Central Banks (ESCB).

December 1995 saw the European Council in Madrid set the framework for banknote and coin production. Euro currency will circulate by January 2002, the exact date announced by the ECB Governing Council before January 1999.

ECOFIN, the European Council of Finance Ministers, entrusted coin production to the Working Group of Mint Directors, consisting of the heads of the National Mints. Eight coins, rising in value from one cent to 2 Euro, will feature in the range. One side of each coin will bear a national design, while the obverse will depict a common pattern.

In June 1997, the Amsterdam European Council endorsed the design for the common side of the coin and invited ECOFIN to adopt the draft Regulation.

Even before the EMI was constituted, long lead times for banknote production led to the committee of the European Central Bank Governors to establish a Working Group on the Printing and Issuing of a European Banknote (BNWG). Comprising Chief Cashiers and General Managers of the NCB printing works, their first decision was to propose a range of seven denominations; 5, 10, 20, 50, 100, 200, and 500.

The EMI Council, on advice from art historians, graphics and marketing experts, selected two themes for a banknote design competition in June 1995; 'Abstract', of the creator's imagination, and 'Ages and Styles of Europe', both bearing the EU flag.

The latter topic represented the architectural history of Europe over distinct periods: Classical, Romanesque, Gothic

Renaissance, Baroque, and Rococo, the Age of Iron and Glass and the 20th Century.

Launched on 12 February 1996, the design competition lasted seven months. After checking for printability and compliance, the NCBs sent the approved designs to a notary in Frankfurt am Main, where a three-digit secret code number replaced authorship identification.

On 20 September 1996, the now anonymous designs were released to the EMI.

A jury of fourteen independent experts from a wide range of disciplines, marketing, art, advertising, etc., representing each EEC country, except Denmark, which had not ratified the Maastrict Treaty, met at the EMI on 26-27 September 1996.

Under the chairmanship of Hanspeter K Scheller, EMI Secretary General, the designs were appraised for creativity, aesthetics, functionality, public perception, avoidance of national bias, and a balance of men and women depicted. Five of each of the two themes provided a shortlist.

Between 7-13 October 1996, Gallup Europe organised a series of focus groups in all EEC countries to evaluate public reaction, consulting 1896 individuals. The results, the jury's appraisal and a technical assessment conducted by the BNWG were submitted to the EMI Council of Governors on 2-3 December 1996.

The winning sketches, in the Ages and Styles of Europe theme, were developed by Robert Kalina of the Oesterreichische Nationalbank. These emphasise windows, gateways and bridges. Blending historical developments, the designs illustrate Europe's common cultural heritage, epitomise the new dawn, and the vision for the future.

On the front, gateways and windows symbolise openness and cooperation. Twelve stars represent the dynamism and harmony of contemporary Europe. Bridges typify European development on the obverse, ranging from pre-Christian constructions to sophisticated suspension bridges, a metaphor for communication among the people of Europe and the world.

Other aspects include the currency name in Latin and Greek, the European flag, the issuing authority initials, BCE, ECB, EZB, EKT, EKP, and the ECB President's signature.

Development of the artwork has been ongoing, turning the winning sketches into sophisticated designs, incorporating the many public and covert security features of a modern banknote.

Dominant colours were chosen by scientific research to assist in recognition. Different note sizes for each denomination with large, bold numerals and tactile features in specific areas were agreed with the European Blind Union to aid the visually impaired.

Modern-day technology offers counterfeiters good results at low cost. To protect banknotes, many security features have been incorporated into the specification.

The paper has fluorescent fibres and both a multitone and barcode watermark, which the forger has difficulty in reproducing. Security thread, intaglio printing and reflective foils are included to help the public.

Several other concealed, machine-readable features enable the NCBs and the note-handling industry to verify authenticity. All aim to detect forgery with a minimum of attention.

Thirteen Member States have printing works. In Belgium, Denmark, Greece, France, Ireland, Italy, Austria and the UK, they are part of the NCB. Finland and Sweden have limited companies wholly owned by their NCB, while Spain has a public company, FNMT.

The Netherlands has a private company, Enschede. Germany's private company is Giesecke & Devrient, Munich and its public company, Bundersdruckerei, Berlin. Portugal buys sheets of partly printed and finishes them itself. Luxembourg sources its banknotes from De La Rue, Gateshead.

These fourteen printers produced nine billion banknotes in 1996, seven billion for domestic use, the rest for issuing authorities outside the EU. With an average life of two years, 12.7 billion banknotes are currently in circulation.

In February 1998, the EMI Council endorsed the final designs together with a full technical specification.

The world awaits the progress of the Euro.

**Editor's note: Researched & written 1999.**

# OTHER BOOKS BY THE AUTHOR

As Good As Gold - History of Pound Sterling. ISBN 0-9534818-4-0

De La Rue Straw Hats to Global Securities. ISBN 0- 9534818-2-4

Euro History & Development. ISBN 0-9534818-1-6
Euro: (eBook): 9781903467145

Holidays 2000 – A Time Capsule. ISBN 0-9534818-7-5

Negotiate to Win! - The Introductory Edition. ISBN 0-9534818-6-7

Start Any Business (Print). ISBN 9781903467008
Start Any Business (eBook). ISBN 9781903467015

Scripophily - Historic Bond & Share Collecting. ISBN  0-9534818-5-9

The Eternal Old Lady - Bank of England. ISBN 0-9534818-3-2

The Green Shoots of Money (Print). ISBN 9781903467107
The Green Shoots of Money (eBook). ISBN 9781903467114

The Hitmen - Part One. ISBN 0-9534818-8-3

# FORTHCOMING BOOKS BY THE AUTHOR

As Good As Gold (Print). ISBN 9781903467039
As Good As Gold (eBook). ISBN 9781903467121

Currants, Olives & Cotton (Print). ISBN 9781903467077
Currants, Olives & Cotton (eBook). ISBN 9781903467169

De La Rue (Print). ISBN 9781903467046
De La Rue (eBook). ISBN 9781903467138

Scripophily (Print). ISBN 9781903467084
Scripophily (eBook). ISBN 9781903467176

Tail-less Cats & Three-legged Men (Print). ISBN 9781903467091
Tail-less Cats & Three-legged Men (eBook). ISBN 9781903467183

The Eternal Old Lady (Print). ISBN 9781903467060
The Eternal Old Lady (eBook). ISBN 9781903467152

## ABOUT THE AUTHOR

Ian Moncrief-Scott has over fifty years of broad business experience, mostly gained at international level, based in the UK.

As a former senior executive for a global publishing and information technology company headquartered in the USA, he has contributed to numerous client-facing procurement and outsourcing initiatives worldwide.

Ian has created and participated in numerous small businesses in the UK, Isle of Man and elsewhere.

He has also represented the Isle of Man Government Department for Enterprise in several of its business support schemes. Ian designed and delivered extensive training for its Micro Business Grant Scheme.

In recognition of his long-term service to the Department, Ian was nominated for The Queen's Award for Enterprise Promotion and awarded an official Certificate of Recognition in 2018.

Throughout his career, he has maintained an active interest in start-ups, especially those involving the financial sector.

At the turn of the millennium, several of the articles written by Ian that form this short work were originally published by the Museum of American Financial History (now the Museum of American Finance).

www.ingramcontent.com/pod-product-compliance
Lightning Source LLC
Chambersburg PA
CBHW042000080526
44588CB00021B/2824